❧ Long for This World

PITT POETRY SERIES

Ed Ochester, *Editor*

Long for This World

NEW AND SELECTED POEMS

Ronald Wallace

University of Pittsburgh Press

The publication of this book
is supported by a grant from the
Pennsylvania Council on the Arts.

Published by the University of Pittsburgh Press,
Pittsburgh, Pa., 15260

10   9   8   7   6   5   4   3   2   1

ISBN 0-8229-5814-7

for my family

❧ Contents

Long for This World: New Poems

1.

2.

Plums, Stones, Kisses & Hooks

(1981)

❧ Installing the Bees

First this: a thousand bees
balled up in one black heart,
a loud wind, a fist of heat,
locked in their thin cage,
edgy with energy.

You carry them out to the hive,
gently, their delicate balance
locked in your dangerous hands,
gorged with your sweet words,
the sky buzzing with dusk.

Then this: the hive like a white thumb
stump on the frozen land.
You open it slowly
and pour the bees out,
as if an escarpment, a sluice.

Now the bees seethe and roil.
You slap down the cover, suddenly
frightened at the weight
that falls from your arms,
the splash of dark waters.

You lift your white hands
to your eyes, waxen, honeyed,
pale lilies, mums, the dead man's
flowers, a thousand bees buzzing
in your wrists.

❧ Oranges

This morning I eat an orange.
It is sour and juicy. My mouth
will tingle all day.
Outside, it is cold. The trees
do not anticipate their leaves.
When I breathe into my hand I smell
oranges.

I walk across the lake.
Ice fishermen twitch their poles until
perch flicker the surface, quick
and bright as orange slices.
The sun ripens in the sky.
The wind turns thin and citrus,
the day precise, fragile.

My mustache and eyelashes freeze.
When I arrive at your house
you are friendly as a fruit seller.
We peel off our clothes, slice through
that wordy rind.
When I lift my fingers to your lips:
oranges.

🐾 One Hook

I knew it was too late
when these blue fish
moved coolly out of the painting.
Klee, what have we done? I said.
But he was fishing, madly fishing.
Make hooks, he said.

Some of the fish slipped smoothly
under the skirts of little girls.
Some hung ties around their necks
and worked for I.B.M.
Some raised hard fins
and swam on highways,
fish mouths honking like horns.

And everything they touched turned
to fish.
The stars wore slime,
the moon grew gills,
trees darted quickly away
in schools.
They ate the grass,
the weeds, the people,
like kelp,
and laid their eggs
while sturgeons in white gowns
came out to round us up.

Klee! Klee! I said. *What is happening?*
What do we do?
But he was fishing,
madly fishing,
Make hooks, he said.

After Being Paralyzed from the Neck Down for Twenty Years, Mr. Wallace Gets a Chin-Operated Motorized Wheelchair

For the first time in twenty years
he is mobile, roaring through corridors,
bouncing off walls, out of control,
breaking doorways, tables, chairs,
and regulations. The hallways stretch out
behind him, startled, amazed,
their plaster and wallpaper gaping,
while somewhere far off,
arms spastically flailing,
the small nurses continue to call:
Mr. Wallace . . . Mr. Wallace . . .

Eventually, he'll listen to reason
and go quietly back to his room,
docile, repentant, and sheepish, promising
not to disappoint them again.
The day shift will sigh and go home.
But, in the evening, between feeding and bedtime,
when they've finally left him alone,
he'll roar over to the corner
and crash through the window
stopping only to watch
the last geese rising,
rising by the light of the snow.

Prayer for Flowers

Show me the disguises of coral root
that I may go unnoticed among enemies,
the tenacity of columbine
that I might thrive in the unlikely place.

Teach me to climb higher than envy,
to trust my own colorful seasons.
Let the wind move me; let me keep my roots.

Like a pitcher plant, let me store up rain
against the dry season, surviving with patience
whatever comes along.
Show me the wind's song through lupine
that my blue days may be filled with music.

Teach me the persistent delicacy of glacier lilies
that I might endure winter's cold, heavy foot.
And, at the end time,
neither stiff-lipped nor trembling,
let me go up, like bear grass,
in a puff of smoke.

❧ Trout

First, slit the belly open
and rinse it clean. Then,
fill it up with butter,
a slab of bacon,
and three fresh slivers of lemon.
Then, wrap it in a skin of foil,
slip it into the coals,
and wait.

When the stars begin to drift toward you
with their thin hooks,
trolling the watery sky,
when the lodgepole pines reel out and in,
resilient, jigging their needles,
when the ground itself,
spawning its dark shadows,
closes its earthy fist,
remove the trout from its burnt pouch,
and eat. The night will settle in,
sweet, the thin air crisp as a fin.

Then, burn the bones
in the last available flame,
take one deep breath, and sleep.
Nothing, now, can haunt you.

FROM

Tunes for Bears to Dance To

(1983)

🐾 Grandmother Grace

I didn't give her a good-bye kiss
as I went off in the bus for the last time,
away from her house in Williamsburg, Iowa,
away from her empty house with Jesus
on all of the walls, with claw-foot tub and sink,
with the angular rooms that trapped all my summers.

I remember going there every summer—
every day beginning with that lavender kiss,
that face sprayed and powdered at the upstairs sink,
then mornings of fragile teacups and old times,
afternoons of spit-moistened hankies and Jesus,
keeping me clean in Williamsburg, Iowa.

Cast off, abandoned, in Williamsburg, Iowa,
I sat in that angular house with summer
dragging me onward, hearing how Jesus
loved Judas despite his last kiss,
how he turned his other cheek time after time,
how God wouldn't let the good person sink.

Months later, at Christmas, my heart would sink
when that flowery letter from Williamsburg, Iowa,
arrived, insistent, always on time,
stiff and perfumed as summer.
She always sealed it with a kiss,
a taped-over dime, and the words of Jesus.

I could have done without the words of Jesus;
the dime was there to make the message sink
in, I thought; and the violet kiss,
quavering and frail, all the way from Williamsburg, Iowa,
sealed some agreement we had for the next summer
as certain and relentless as time.

I didn't know this would be the last time.
If I had, I might even have prayed to Jesus
to let me see her once again next summer.
But how could I know she would sink,
her feet fat boats of cancer, in Williamsburg, Iowa,
alone, forsaken, without my last kiss?

I was ten, Jesus, and the idea of a kiss
at that time made my young stomach sink.
Let it be summer. Let it be Williamsburg, Iowa.

❧ The Belly Dancer in the Nursing Home

The crazy ladies are singing again,
clapping their hands and gums to the music,
dancing their wheelchairs to and fro
with a frail and bony toe.
In the front row, some old men,
flushed with the heat of the season,
are thumping their tuneless canes and stumps,
driving old age and infirmity
out of the room like an unwanted guest.
Meanwhile, the belly dancer,
all sweat and sequins, muscles and skin,
ripples and pumps,
her skimpy metallic costume slipping
beneath her secret hair,
until even my father, slumped in his chair,
lifts his voice and quickens:
Goddamn! he sings. *Look there!*
Until we're all dancing and singing,
hips, breasts, and heads ringing
the immodest, unlikely air,
until the performance is over.
The women stiffen into their chairs;
the men lean back on their silence;
and my father folds up as in prayer,
with just enough breath left to whisper.
And sing. And dance. And swear.

The Assistant Professor's Nightmare

I'm giving the Faulkner lecture as usual,
all the pencils nodding their heads
in astonishment: Wallace is brilliant,
Wallace is wise. My sure voice filling
their notebooks up when
back row, aisle three, Kevin McGann,
graduate teaching assistant, begins
to shake his ominous head. A white balloon
drifts out of his mouth, and oozes
to the front of the room: *ridiculous,*
it says, *ridiculous.* Suddenly confidence
slips out of my voice, sits down
in the front row snoring.
My stomach and the room give out,
my small words stumbling on. Soon
all of the pencils are wagging their fingers,
shouting with their black tongues.
Two hundred points rise up at me
as I grow smaller and smaller, my thin
voice humming like a gnat. I look
for a safe way out of this, but
lost in grammatical confusion,
my sentence goes on and on
and I disappear in a flurry of notes,
my fury and my sound crossed out,
the room closed up like a book.

❦ A Hot Property

I am not. I am
an also-ran,
a bridesmaid, a finalist,
a second-best bed. I am
the one they could just
as easily have given it to
but didn't.
I'm a near miss, a close second,
an understudy, a runner-up.
I'm the one who was just
edged, shaded, bested, nosed out.
I made the final cut,
the short list,
the long deliberation.
I'm good, very good,
but I'm not good enough.
I'm an alternate, a backup,
a very close decision,
a red ribbon, a handshake,
a glowing commendation.
You don't know me.
I've a dozen names,
all honorably mentioned.
I could be anybody.

"You Can't Write a Poem about McDonald's"

Noon. Hunger the only thing
singing in my belly.
I walk through the blossoming cherry trees
on the library mall,
past the young couples coupling,
by the crazy fanatic
screaming doom and salvation
at a sensation-hungry crowd,
to the Lake Street McDonald's.
It is crowded, the lines long and sluggish.
I wait in the greasy air.
All around me people are eating—
the sizzle of conversation,
the salty odor of sweat,
the warm flesh pressing out of
hip-huggers and halter tops.
When I finally reach the cash register,
the counter girl is crisp as a pickle,
her fingers thin as french fries,
her face brown as a bun.
Suddenly I understand cannibalism.
As I reach for her,
she breaks into pieces
wrapped neat and packaged for take-out.
I'm thinking, how amazing it is
to live in this country, how easy
it is to be filled.
We leave together, her warm aroma
close at my side.
I walk back through the cherry trees
blossoming up into pies,

the young couples frying in
the hot, oily sun,
the crowd eating up the fanatic,
singing, my ear, eye, and tongue
fat with the wonder
of this hungry world.

❧ Picture of Molly, Age 4

Picture this: a child with eyes as blue
as the first blue scylla of spring,
hair the color of oak leaves in the fall,
a voice as pure as bloodroot, and as clear.
A small bud of surprises;
a wildflower of light;
a poem you wish you had written,
and will take all the credit for.
In short, a child so beautiful
she could only be your own,
telling a friend outside your study door,
You can't read his books because
there are too many words
and there aren't any pictures at all.

🦇 1001 Nights

Each night I read you stories—
Sinbad, Aladdin, Periebanou, Periezade—
in that strange exotic language
you cannot possibly understand:
countenance, repast, bequeathed, nuptial,
what can these words be telling you?
What can they signify?
That I love you? That it's time to sleep?
Keep safe throughout this night?
And yet you will not let me simplify,
get angry if I explain,
and hang on every word as if
our lives depended on it.
Perhaps they do.
One day the stories will fail us,
there will be nothing left to tell,
another hand will rub your back,
another genie will rise.
But for now, sleep tight, sleep tight,
and dream of the singing tree,
the speaking bird, the golden water,
the stone that was your father
restored by morning light.

❧ The Facts of Life

She wonders how people get babies.
Suddenly vague and distracted,
we talk about "making love."
She's six and unsatisfied, finds
our limp answers unpersuasive.
Embarrassed, we stiffen, and try again,
this time exposing the stark naked words:
penis, vagina, sperm, womb, and *egg.*
She thinks we're pulling her leg.
We decide that it's time
to get passionate and insist.
But she's angry, disgusted.
Why do we always make fun of her?
Why do we lie?
We sigh, try cabbages, storks.
She smiles. *That's more like it.*
We talk on into the night, trying
magic seeds, good fairies, God . . .

FROM

People and Dog in the Sun

(1987)

❧ The Nude Gardener

Surrounded by burdock and foxtail
on the hillside behind the house
you dig up a would-be garden,
nude except for your shoes.

Inside, I watch your breasts swing
as you bend to your work,
your buttocks slightly puckered
with strain and middle age.

Your leg to the spade, your hand
shading your eyes, you gaze
somewhere into the far trees
and smile. What do you see?

Is it the neighboring farmer
falling off his tractor in amazement?
The mailman on his rural rounds
handed a package he'll deliver

to every friend in town?
The farmer's son, fourteen, coon
hunting, as he's told his mom
every day this week?

Or is it something farther off,
more ancient than the trees,
that tingles on your skin
and makes my married knees

weaker with anticipation
than for years they've been?
Weeds fall off the hillside
and you are standing in

coneflower, hollyhock, bergamot,
blossoming with wild abandon!

❧ This Night

Seated beside them,
squeezing the rubbery teats,
breathing to the ping of the milk stream,
I can almost forget
how anyone could want
anything other than this:
the horses shifting softly in the stalls,
the eight cats arranged politely
around the tin of skimmed-off milk,
the Nubians on their regal platforms,
queens of the field and feed bin.

Until I dream the whole world eating,
the universe dreamily eating,
as, under the hungry stars,
the night closes its great beak,
and a barn owl's wheezy shriek
detonates the light,
as if this were the last night
for us all,
and not just any night.

🐾 At Chet's Feed & Seed

The man who is telling me about the chicken
stationery he makes in his backyard trailer
leaves with his beaky wife.
Their voices clabber and scratch.
In the corner, guinea hens, $1.50 each,
scutter and strut in jerky grandeur.
Clyde is pleased to meet me. He
shakes my hand, a 200 lb. feed bag
perched on his left shoulder, his big
arm, glistening in its sleeveless T-shirt,
a mixture of roast corn, oats, molasses, wheat.
The bald woman tied up to her chihuahua,
her son still in Vietnam with the Marines,
adjusts her rheumy teeth.
She says he'll be coming back.
Chet says he will, pulls a pencil out of his ear
and takes a dollar off her bill.
She grunts. Chet bleats at Clyde
who whinnies under the weight of the feed sack.
The chicken man and his wife come back.
They're looking at me.
The smell of feed and goodwill is sweet.
I feel so stupid I could almost moo
with approval. So I do.

🐾 Poem Written Mostly by Fourth Graders

They're all here, exactly where we left them
so many years ago, familiar as sonnets,
the thumb-suckers and small sprawlers,
the bed-wetters, best friends, and bullies,
grouped on the grade school auditorium risers
in their pigtails and crew cuts,
their headbands and braces,
their cub scout belts and tennies,
their inimitable swaggers and grins.
Here's the girl with her pants snap open,
the boy excavating his nose,
here's the fat kid with bottle-thick
glasses, his shirt buttoned up to his neck,
gawking at nothing at all. And yet

who are these strangers who march up one by one,
a bouquet of stiff papers clutched in their hands,
to make humpback whales wash up in Wisconsin,
dogs take ballet and play baseball and soccer,
sunfish rise and set and tell jokes under water?
Who told them that gray is a suitcase or a gray
moldy carrot, that blue doesn't argue
but despises black, that people who turn into possums
eat eggshells, that a girl, dressed in red,
reading a poem about red
and how her face turns red
when she feels foolish, turns red?
Behind me, a grandmother says, "Back in my time
these weren't called poems. They don't even rhyme!"

While beside me my five-year-old starry-eyed daughter
shouts, "That was great one!" up to her nine-year-old sister
and brings the house down
as the air fills with dolphins of laughter,

a ripple of whistles and clicks
finning through waves of applause.
So the laws of nostalgia are broken
as our children and childhoods threaten
to sail off without and beyond us
into their own strange lands,
until the moth-eaten red curtain closes,
the thumb-suckers and sprawlers return like a tide,
and we take them, small wonders, bright charms,
in the nets of our metrical arms.

🐝 Matheny

Remember me? The class jack-off.
In ninth grade I ripped up
a whole row of bolted-down school desks
and threw them out the music room window.
You applauded. You egged me on. I'd do
everything you wanted to but wouldn't:
throb spitwads at the teacher,
snap any girl's bra strap,
blow farts on my naked arm.

M'weenie! you called out. *M'weenie!*
I took the heat, paid the piper, faced
the music, while you,
getting your rocks off, looked on.
Now who's the failure? You
with your teacup hands,
your bald smiles and small promotions?
Or me, Matheny, the flunky, the great
debunker. Your drab imagination's ingot.
The gold in your memory's coffer.

❧ Nightline: An Interview with the General

The retired general is talking about restraint,
how he could have blown them all to kingdom come.
Read between the lines: this man's a saint.

War is, after all, not for the faint-
hearted. It's more than glory, fife, and drum,
and tired generals talking of restraint.

Make no mistake. He's never been one to paint
a rosy picture, mince words, or play dumb.
Caught behind the lines no man's a saint.

But why should strong offensives ever taint
a country pressed by Leftist, Red, and Hun?
He's generally tired of talking about restraint,

tired of being muzzled by every constraint
put on him. He thinks the time has come
to draw the line between the devil and the saint,

to silence protest, demonstration, and complaint,
beneath a smooth, efficient, military hum.
The general's retired all talk of restraint.
He aligns himself with God. And God's no saint.

❧ People and Dog in the Sun

Summer: to the lakefront the old people
come, walking their whimsical dogs.
Each year when the sentimental sun
comes back to admire its face in the water,
these twosomes return: the old
story of loneliness and love. And each time

I see them, awkwardly rocking in time
to the same broken song, they seem less like people
than like strange haunted vessels—old
boats that all winter have gone to the dogs
until now, here, beside the bright water,
they drift in the westering sun.

"There's nothing new under the sun,"
one of them tells me this time.
"You'd think they could walk on water,"
she goes on about those "terrible people"
who think they're her betters, who continually dog
the poor, the unfortunate, the old.

And I wonder what it's like to be old
in this country: A meandering walk in the sun,
some small talk in the company of a dog
one's last best hope of a good time.
I think how different it must be for these people
so near death, their names written on water.

Such thoughts, I know, won't hold water.
Most ways, I suppose, even the very old
are like anyone else. People are people.
No matter the season, the sun is the sun.
And further, there is something about the times
hanging around us *all* like an old dog,

some dark, irremediable hunger. Miro's dog
dreams a man from its head, the gray air thick as water.
His small boy blaring by is a clock racing time,
his woman a mushroom that will never grow old,
his whole portrait the color of the sun.
What do we make of these people?

If time disappears in a fury of sun,
if we all, old and young, become so much vaporized water,
may some sly dog live on, whimsically dreaming up people.

FROM

The Makings of Happiness

(1991)

🐛 Early Brass

for Emily

When five balding men in long-tailed tuxedos
rise to the bright occasion, their brass
sacbuts, cornet, and slide trumpet in hand, O
the chansons and canzoni, the madrigals, the sass
they pull out of their bold embouchures! Their bravado's
a coinage of lieder and light so daft
no music could, under sweet heaven, surpass
the New York Cornet & Sacbut Ensemble's.

Yet last night in the lunchroom of Van Hise School,
when my sixth-grade daughter and her oversized trombone—
all silverware, sour milk, and John Philip Sousa—
sashayed on stage at a slapstick recital,
she sounded (by God!) not altogether un-
like the New York Cornet & Sacbut Ensemble.

🐾 Bluegills

Fast in the wire mesh basket
tied to the dock, six bluegills,
duped by dazzle and subterfuge,
shimmer and flick. My daughter,
reeling in my permission,
is about to let them out.
Oh, don't, her great-aunts shout,
that's money in the bank, that's dinner.
Out in the bay a great blue
heron rudders and swoops,
scooping up light and silver.

It's a stand-off: my poor daughter
poised on the dock; my aunts,
hackles up, in a fluster;
the rich fish slipping
from their narrow enclosure;
and me, who only wants everybody
happy, on this bright day
getting darker, eating my words
as if that could save
anyone, cast off
the world's great hunger.

🐟 Fresh Oysters & Beer

I'm lifting the oysters
up from the ice chips,
scooping the slippery pap
loose with a spoon,
dripping the sliver of lemon, the ripe
island of tabasco, and then
flipping it all up to my lip and sipping
it in, the rough texture of shell
on incisor, the limp liquidy tongue
poised for the pleasure
of soft palate and swallow, and
the following chilled schooner of beer.
Meanwhile, my rampantly
adolescent daughter, vegetarian and
teetotaler, is squirming, her frown
brown and decaying on her face.
She's eating her breadsticks
and lettuce, the tofu and lentils
she's smuggled in under her sweatshirt,
a bundle of grimace and disgust.
Can't we see, she screams, *that's
a creature!* as the patrons of happy
hour turn toward us, and the taste-
fully well-endowed waitresses
in their wet T-shirts emblazoned
"I got the crabs at Cap'n Curt's"
stop to scratch their saucy behinds.
A creature! she shrieks, exasperated,
as Cap'n Curt sticks his head
out of the sizzling kitchen, rolls
the oyster-like whites of his eyes
at the fat bouncer in the far corner,

who gets up slowly and comes toward us,
as I flip a bill from my wallet,
and we exit, meek as vegetables,
me and my steamy daughter
just so much meat in his eyes.

⚜ Off the Record

In the attic I find the notes
he kept in college
over forty years ago: *Hooray*
for Thanksgiving vacation! he wrote
in the margin of Psych 102.
And for a moment I can see him there,

feel the exuberance surge through
that odd cell of his body
where I am still
a secret code uncompleted, a piece
of DNA, some ancient star-stuff.
And then I find a recording of me

from 1948, when he was twenty-two
and I was three, and I can see,
from my perch up on his shoulders,
him stopping at the gaudy arcade,
plugging his lucky quarter into
the future where we'd always be.

Maybe imagination is just
a form of memory after all, locked
deep in the double helix of eternity.
Or maybe the past is but one more
phantasmagoric invention we use
to fool ourselves into someone else's shoes.

It is not my voice I want to hear
on memory's fading page, on imagination's disk.
It is my father's in the background
prompting me, doing his best
to stay off the record, his hushed
instructions vanishing in static.

🐾 Fan Mail

When Marjorie, the information manager
of a chin-operated wheelchair company,
writes to say how much she liked my poem
about a *Mr. Wallace* who, paralyzed from
the neck down for twenty years, when
he got his first motorized wheelchair,
roared around the nursing home, caroming
off walls, tearing up linoleum, leaving
his mark on things again, making an
impression he hadn't made for years,
and finally crashed (figuratively, perhaps)
out the fourth-floor picture window
of his recuperating room,
and sailed off in slow motion
trailing bright stars of glass,
and tells me she, too, has been paralyzed
from the neck down for so long she'd
thought her funny bone as well had gone,

I think about you again, Father, slumped
in the vast doorway of the past, grinning
under the weight of a frame grown huge
on you, and how we sat those distant afternoons
in urine smell and silence, waiting
for the night nurse to lay you
one last time on that taut bed.
And so, when, in this chin-operated missive,
its five good-tempered sentences
tapped out with what intensive care, Marjorie
says if my *Mr. Wallace* is someone real I know
and love, and think could use her company,
then I should send her his address so

she can get in touch (there have been
such developments!), although it's been
ten years since you on this hard earth
have had a local habitation, I lift my chin.
I send this exultation in your name.

🜚 The Hell Mural: Panel I

Iri and Toshi Maruki are "painting the bomb."
Their painting, they say, will comfort the souls of the dead.
"It's a dreadful cruel scene of great beauty,"
Toshi says. "The face may be deformed but there's kindness
in a finger or a breast, even in hell."
The Hell Mural spreads over the floor.

Iri stretches naked on the floor,
painting. He remembers Hiroshima after the bomb—
the bodies stacked up, arms outstretched toward hell,
nothing he could see that was not dead,
nothing that cared at all for human kindness,
nothing that wept at such terror, such beauty.

Now a brush stroke here, a thick wash there, and beauty
writhes and stretches from the canvas floor.
He wants his art to "collaborate with kindness,"
he wants his art to "uncover the bomb."
But no lifetime's enough to paint all the dead
or put all those who belong there in hell.

"Hitler and Truman," he says, "of course are in hell.
But even those of us who live for beauty
are in hell, no less so than the dead."
(He paints himself and Toshi on the floor.)
"All of us who cannot stop the bomb
are now in hell. It's no kindness

to say different. It's no kindness
to insist on heaven; there's only hell."
Toshi adds bees and maggots to the bomb,
and birds, cats, her pregnant niece, the beauty
of severed breast and torn limb on the killing floor.
"In Hiroshima," she says, "we crossed a river on the dead

bodies stacked up like a bridge. Now the dead
souls must be comforted with kindness.
Come walk in your socks across our floor,
walk on the canvas. (A little dirt in hell
almost improves it.) Can you see the beauty
of this torso, that ear lobe, this hip bone of the bomb?"

Iri and Toshi Maruki, in "Hell," are painting the bomb,
the mural on their floor alive with the thriving dead.
Come walk on their kindness, walk on their troublesome beauty.

🦌 Building an Outhouse

Is not unlike building a poem: the pure
mathematics of shape; the music of hammer
and tenpenny nail, of floor joist, stud wall,
and sill; the cut wood's sweet smell.

If the Skil saw rear up in your unpracticed hand,
cussing, hawking its chaw of dust,
and you're lost in the pounding particulars
of fly rafters, siding, hypotenuse, and load,
until nothing seems level or true
but the scorn of the tape's clucked tongue,

let the nub of your plainspoken pencil prevail
and it's up! Functional. Tight as a sonnet.
It will last forever (or at least for a while)
though the critics come sit on it, and sit on it.

🦋 In the Amish Bakery

I don't know why what comes to mind
when I imagine my wife and daughters,
off on a separate vacation
in the family car,
crashing—no survivors—
in one of those godless snowstorms
of Northern Illinois,
is that Amish bakery
in Sauk County, Wisconsin, where,
on Saturday mornings in summer,
we used to go—
all powdered sugar and honey in
the glazed caramel air. And O
the browned loaves rising,
the donuts, buns, and pies, the ripe
strawberry stain of an oven burn
on the cheek of one of the wives.
And outside in the yard
that trampoline
where we'd imagine them—
the whole blessed family in
their black topcoats and frocks,
their severe hair and beards,
their foolish half-baked grins,
so much flour dust and leaven—
leaping all together on
their stiff sweet legs toward heaven.

🐾 The Fat of the Land

Gathered in the heavy heat of Indiana,
summer and 102°, we've come from
all over this great country,
one big happy family, back from
wherever we've spread ourselves too thin.
A cornucopia of cousins and uncles, grand-
parents and aunts, nieces and nephews, expanding.
All day we laze on the oily beach;
we eat all the smoke-filled evening:
shrimp dip and crackers,
Velveeta cheese and beer,
handfuls of junk food, vanishing.
We sit at card tables, examining
our pudgy hands, piling in
hot fudge and double chocolate
brownies, strawberry shortcake and cream,
as the lard-ball children
sluice from room to room.
O the loveliness of so much loved flesh,
the litany of split seams and puffed sleeves,
sack dresses and Sansabelt slacks,
dimpled knees and knuckles, the jiggle
of triple chins. O the gladness
that only a family understands,
our fat smiles dancing
as we play our cards right.
Our jovial conversation blooms and booms
in love's large company, as our sweet
words ripen and split their skins:
mulberry, fabulous, flotation,
phlegmatic, plumbaginous.
Let our large hearts attack us,

our blood run us off the scale.
We're huge and whole on this simmering night,
battened against the small skinny
futures that must befall all of us,
the gray thin days and the noncaloric dark.

FROM

Time's Fancy

(1994)

🐦 The Life Next at Hand

Behind a camouflage of sticks and debris
we once mistook for a sparrow's routine intrusions
a house wren is building
her nest in the Shopper Stopper box.
Every day when the mailman,
driving, left-handed, his beater,
leans as far into her life as he can,
she gives him what-for in a song.

I have reached in more than once myself
to pull some tiresome sparrow out
of a place meant for something better
before I've found that small cup of promises—
a puff of the tiniest grasses, a twist of snakeskin—
behind the wordy camouflage of the commonplace.

❧ Why I Am Not a Nudist
for Margaret, August 3, 1993

Mornings, I like to lie in bed
feigning sleep as my wife rises,
pads to the bathroom on her bare feet
in the rhythm that,
after twenty-five years of marriage,
I know by heart.

I like to watch, surreptitious,
my eyes still thick with sleep, her slip
out of her prim wool nightshirt,
and into her cotton panties—the half
knee-bend she does to pull them straight—
and the way her small breasts flatten
as she rears back and crosses her arms
to pull her T-shirt over.

She pretends not to know I watch her,
or how the still small pleasure
of the withheld sweet familiar
stays mysterious after all.
And if the day begins to fray
from grace toward consternation—
all that naked bickering—
imagination's raiment stays inviolate.

It is perhaps not unlike how what you
maybe once engaged in—in the heat
of passion, say, some small unspeakable
kinkiness you could hardly believe
you'd think of, and could not consider
afterwards without embarrassment,
that nevertheless provided
such unlikely mutual pleasure—
must remain secret.

❧ A Valentine

after Heisenberg

It is just good physics
how, merely by observing,
the observer changes the observed.
Not that I know much about physics,

but maybe the human heart
works on the same principle.
When William Harvey, the principle
discoverer of the heart's

motion, posited the pump
as metaphor, the poet
and scientist merged, and the poet
changed forever both pump

and heart. I am no scientist,
but Love, look at this pump,
this heart; it pumps
for you sure as a scientist

changes the whole world
with his patient, loving
observations, sure as you, loving
me, would change the whole world.

❧ The Story

When we came out to the island
we didn't expect . . . ah,
that would be the way to begin:
a half-sentence of promise and mystery,
the delicious delay of gratification
at the end of each
anticipatory line; *When . . .*
the Western time frame, fixed, dependable,
with all its philosophical trappings—
cause and effect, progress, the idea
of heaven; *We . . .*
the invention of the self, the romantic
fiction of the individual, within
democracy's improbable community; *Came . . .*
the active verb, graphic, decisive,
encoded with sexual reference; *Out . . .*
a kind of emergence, perhaps?
leaving the safety of the shore
and our old lives behind? *To . . .*
that innocent preposition with its
homonymal undercurrents that
tripped our childhoods up; *The . . .*
the almost invisible modifier,
incontrovertible article
of faith in the solidity and
particularity of things; *Island . . .*
the exotic setting, would it be
South Seas? or North Atlantic?
That self-contained isolating boundary
the tides ravish daily with their
intriguing cargo; *We . . .*
and by now we're friends,
dear reader, aren't we? The child's
thrill of excitement and abandon

in that ecstatic syllable; *Didn't* . . .
the off-handed contraction, informal,
conversational, masking its bipolar
opposites—assertion and negation,
push and pull, give and take,
the yes and no, the death that
defines the entrance; *Expect* . . .
and isn't that the heart of any story,
after all? Expectation and desire
the energy that attends every journey,
the gas that fuels the lobster boat,
the wind that fills the sails,
the sea that keeps us afloat toward . . .
What! the mind, hankering after arrivals,
keeps shouting through the morning fog.
Although it knows to know
the answer is
to kill the story off,
close it down so tight
no light or breath can enter,
leaving it, and us, no place
to go, yet it will
drive on regardless to its ending,
will demand to know.

❧ The Swing

How could he know that that
moment, strung between his parents'
hands like some improbable bead, or part
of a chain that, for all he knew, extended
indefinitely into a world that seemed
large and untarnishable, would stay
fixed in his memory more surely than
any occasion of real moment. That
the definition of "momentous" would, in fact,
change as he aged down the years, spinning
the dross of his childhood to gold.
That his father would, eventually,
as all things eventually must, rust
through, and break his hold on him
and his mother fray and snap
like the strand of nylon wiring
a cheap string of pearls, leaving him flat-
footed on the cracked sidewalk,
he who had swung free of gravity and time
in that one moment when he was too
giddy in the thin air of his
childhood even to notice.

And now in the days long with thought,
that kid has no use for him, isn't about
to stop his ascent into the heavens
he knows surely are there, as surely as
this moment, his moment,
will last at least forever.

✤ Hardware

My father always knew the secret
name of everything—
stove bolt and wing nut,
set screw and rasp, ratchet
wrench, band saw, and ball
peen hammer. He was my
tour guide and translator
through that foreign country
with its short-tempered natives
in their crew cuts and tattoos,
who suffered my incompetence
with gruffness and disgust.
Pay attention, he would say,
and you'll learn a thing or two.

Now it's forty years later,
and I'm packing up his tools
*(If you know the proper
names of things you're never
at a loss)* tongue-tied, incompetent,
my hands and heart full
of doohickeys and widgets,
watchamacallits, thingamabobs.

🪲 Pantoum: The Sturdy of Worry

In the paper today I read [sic]
about "a sturdy of worry"
at the local psychiatric clinic.
They are prepared to pay money

to study the sturdy who worry
though there's nothing to worry about.
If they're prepared to pay money,
I'll sign up. I worry a lot.

Though there's nothing to worry about,
I'm continually sick to my stomach.
Signing up to worry—my lot
in life. No confidence. No pluck.

I'm continually sick to my stomach.
Meet anxiety, my oldest friend,
Mr. No Confidence, Mr. No Pluck.
But what if my anxiety ends?

If anxiety, my oldest friend,
at the local psychiatric clinic,
ends? *What if my anxiety ends?*
I read today's paper, worried sick.

𝕏 Why God Permits Evil

At age eleven he seriously considered
cutting the hair from his sister's Barbie
and pasting it strategically on his pubes
to look in the sixth-grade locker room
more like a man. Instead, he hid in a corner,
and slipped from his obligatory jockstrap
straight into his stained BVDs
as the rest of us paraded in the showers
with what must have looked to him
like steel wool, woven mats, thatch.

Did he know we needed him?
Would always need someone like him?

It's not unlike the argument for why
God permits evil, without which who
could know or choose the good?
We've all been that small boy
stuck in the corner, assaulted by
the catcalls, hoots, and whistles,
which may explain the secret joy we feel
when the rich grow poor, the mighty fall,
and we give them all the sympathy
and comfort we can muster
across our phony faces.

❧ Ballade of the Humpback Whales

Here, in the Atlantic, off the coast
at Provincetown, we've come to see the whales
antic and cavort through the long feast
days of midsummer. Off the boat's prow, schools
of dolphins shimmer and pitch, arched like sails
in the whitecaps, while up on deck, wind-
blown and ruddy, fat as cable spools,
giddy with the songs of humpback whales,

we sight the first spout in the distance
mounting its airy plume toward heaven. Smells
of salt and tuna swim up from the East
as the spokesman for the Cetacean Institute tells
about the invisible drifting nets that spell
trouble for us all, how, entangled, bound
for Mexico to spawn, ill-fed, still
giddy with their songs, the humpback whales

will starve. But there, off the bow, our first
humpback is lob-tailing, a gay carousel
of plash and sparkle, while another, flippers poised,
dives deep, and soars up in a breach, the swell
slapping us silly, our large hearts, bell-
like, clanging, our own loud voices finned
with wonder. Our spokesman goes on to tell
us how, giddy with a song, one humpback whale

will teach it to another and another until
the whole great sea is filled with lovely sound.
God give us the good music and the will
to sing along, giddy, with the humpback whales.

🎋 Teachers: A Primer

Mrs. Goldwasser

   Shimmered like butterscotch; the sun
   had nothing on her. She bangled
   when she walked. No one
   did not love her. She shone,
   she glowed, she lit up any room,
   her every gesture jewelry.
   And O, when she called us all by name
   how we all performed!

   Her string of little beads,
   her pearls, her rough-cut
   gemstones, diamonds, we hung
   about her neck. And when
   the future pressed her flat,
   the world unclasped, and tarnished.

Mrs. Sands

   Always dressed in tan. Her voice
   abrasive as her name. What choice
   did a second-grader have? You got
   what you got. Her room was hot
   but she wore wool and heavy sweat
   and worked our childhoods, short and sweet.
   You didn't sass her or the school or
   she'd rap your knuckles with a ruler.

   She had a policy: A tattletale
   or liar had to face the wall,
   a tail pinned to his sorry ass,
   and wear the laughter of the class.
   So, to this day, my knuckles bent,
   I tell the truth (but tell it slant).

Mrs. Orton

The perennial substitute, like some
obnoxious weed, a European interloper
in our native prairie, her instructions
full of nettles, her gestures parsnip
and burdock. Every day at 3:00 P.M.
we'd dig her out of our small lives,
and every morning she'd pop back.
We prayed she'd get the sack.

And to that end we taunted her—
tacks on her chair, a set-back clock—
as, weeping, she plodded through the week
turning, and turning the other cheek.
And every time we thought that we'd
eradicated her, she'd gone to seed.

Miss Willingham

A Southern Belle, she read *Huck Finn*
aloud to us, dropping her chin
to get the accent right. And me,
for some odd reason, she
singled out to learn the books
of the Bible and recite them back
to her in my high voice
I tried to measure lower. *Nice*

boys go to Sunday School, she said,
and made me promise, when I was grown,
to glorify our heavenly Lord
and take His teaching for my own.
And when she finished that dull story,
she lit out for the territory.

Mr. Axt

The basketball coach. Short, tough.
Three days' growth on his sharp chin.
Liked to see us all play rough,
and beat up on the stupid, thin,
weak kids who couldn't take it.
He wore white T-shirts, shoes, and slacks,
and taught us all to fake it
if we somehow naturally lacked
the mean competitive spirit.
Once a week he'd have us
bend over and spread our cheeks
for him and old Doc Moffett
who liked to slap us on the butt
and watch as we took leaks.

Mrs. Replogle

Her name forbidding, reptilian,
her reputation like a snake
around my expectations.
But then she played Swan Lake
and Ferde Grofé's Grand Canyon Suite,
a Bach chorale, a Beethoven quartet,
and when we were all back on the street
even the traffic kept a beat.

One day she had us close our eyes
and listen to a symphony
and write whatever image rose
in our small imagination's dark.
And what I saw was poetry,
each note a bird, a flower, a spark.

Mr. Glusenkamp

His gray face was a trapezoid, his voice
droned on like an ellipse.
He hated students and their noise
and loved the full eclipse
of their faces at the end of the day.
No one could have been squarer,
and nothing could have been plainer
than his geometry.

He didn't go for newfangled
stuff—new math, the open classroom.
And yet he taught us angles
and how lines intersect and bloom,
and how infinity was no escape,
and how to give abstractions shape.

Mr. Watts

Sat cross-legged on his desk,
a pretzel of a man, and grinned
as if chemistry were some cosmic joke
and he'd been dealt a hand
of wild cards, all aces.
He drew for us a "ferrous" wheel
and showed when formic acid reverses
HCOOH becomes HOOCH, a peal
of laughter ringing from his nose.
He gave us Avogadro's number
and in his stained lab clothes
formulas for blowing the world asunder
or splitting genes. God knows
why he died shouting "No!" in thunder.

Miss Goff

When Zack Pulanski brought the plastic vomit
and slid it slickly to the vinyl floor
and raised his hand, and her tired eyes fell on it
with horror, the heartless classroom lost in laughter
as the custodian slyly tossed his sawdust on it
and pushed it, grinning, through the door,
she reached into her ancient corner closet
and found some Emily Dickinson mimeos there

which she passed out. And then, herself
passed out on the cold circumference of her desk.
And everybody went their merry ways
but me, who, chancing on one unexpected phrase
after another, sat transfixed until dusk.
Me and Miss Goff, the top of our heads taken off.

❧ In the Cards

Midnight. She complains
in the nursing home they
play too slow, forget what's
led, make up their own rules,
cheat. My grandmother, 89, abloom
in her flower-print dress and Ben
Hogan golf cap, her tinted gray
spectacles and cane, her sensible
shoes, reviews the sleepy bidding.
She's waited all year for this:
her children sprawled around her
at the table one last time,
their scores climbing brightly
on the score pad.

Wide awake for once, she exclaims
how she's amazed by each new day,
her one blind eye a pool
of blue glacier water, her other
eye asquint and smiling, her lips
blue in this warm room, taking
tricks for all she's worth.
The evening blurs into beer,
smoke, Velveeta, and sleep.
Oh my, she remarks, *hearts
are trump?* And they are,
and we hold the cards she's dealt us,
and we make our startled bids,
or go over, or go down.

❧ Grandfather, His Book

When my maternal grandfather turned ninety-one,
he took my mother's Underwood and began
to type out the mad story of his life, and,
though he'd never learned to type, roared on
for thirty-some odd days, exhausting one
ream of paper after another, smiling
at the indecipherable gibberish on the page
as if he'd found a reason for his old age.

And if my mother wept, she nevertheless
bound that story together and passed it on
to anyone at the funeral who might one
day make something of it, more or less,
while Grandfather lay, smiling at the pews
where all his family sat like good reviews.

The Uses of Adversity

(1998)

❧ The Friday Night Fights

Every Friday night we watched the fights.
Me, ten years old and stretched out on the couch;
my father, in his wheelchair, looking on
as Rocky Marciano, Sonny Liston, Floyd Patterson
fought and won the battles we could not.
Him, twenty-nine, and beat up with disease;
me, counting God among my enemies
for what he'd done to us. We never touched.

But in between the rounds we'd sing how we'd
Look sharp! Feel sharp! & Be sharp! with Gillette
and Howard Cosell, the Bela Lugosi of boxing.
Out in the kitchen, my mother never understood
our need for blood, how this was as close as we'd get
to love—bobbing and weaving, feinting and sparring.

🐝 Fielding

I like to see him out in center field
fifty years ago, at twenty-two,
waiting for that towering fly ball—
August, Williamsburg, a lazy afternoon—
dreaming how he'd one day be a pro
and how he'd have a wide-eyed son to throw
a few fat pitches to. An easy catch.
He drifts back deeper into a small patch

of weeds at the fence and waits. In a second or two
the ball is going to stagger in the air,
the future take him to his knees: wheelchair,
MS, paralysis, grief. But for now
he's camped out under happiness. Life is good.
For at least one second more he owns the world.

❦ Tonight's Lecture: The Effects of Head Wounds on Foot Soldiers, A Case Study

Government scientists are experimenting with cats
to determine the effects of head wounds on foot soldiers. The cats
are strapped to special tables, their heads in a vise,
and shot with military assault rifles. The effects
are noticeable. Without their heads, the cats become dis-
oriented, have trouble breathing, and no longer function
fully as cats. The government scientists speculate
that head-wounded foot soldiers experience similar discomfort.

The cats are kept in cages for observation.
They lose their appetites and often become depressed,
reflecting post-traumatic stress syndrome as well.
The lecturer stops. The congressmen are incredulous,
shake their collective heads. *War is hell!* They'll
approve the development of better headgear for foot soldiers.

🦃 Panties

His wife says women simply don't wear "panties."
"Briefs," she says, or "underwear," or maybe
"underpants," or even, these days, "Jockeys."
But the only "panties" women wear are in men's
imaginations. Her friends agree, though one says
she's seen "panties" in a Victoria's Secret catalogue.
My case is closed, his wife says. *Men like to og-*
le women in language as well as in person.

He'd used the word in a poem about his wife
that subsequently appeared in a review in the local paper
for all her friends to see. Never in her life
had she been so embarrassed. Now everyone would gape or
smirk at her. But he's lost in his fantasies,
parading there before them in his panties.

🐜 The Bad Sonnet

It stayed up late, refused to go to bed,
and when it did it sang loud songs instead
of sleeping, disturbing its siblings—couplets, quatrains
in their small rooms, began caterwauling—
and soon the whole neighborhood was awake.
Sometimes it got in petty trouble with the law,
shoplifting any little thing it saw
that caught its fancy: happiness and heartache

slipped neatly in its pocket. It joined a gang
that forged currency, bombed conventions, and finally
tried to bump off all its competition.
Through a sequence of events, luckily
it was caught, handcuffed, and taken off to jail
where it would not keep quiet in its cell.

L=A=N=G=U=A=G=E

The poet says that language is an absence,
and a *beautiful* absence, at that. Representation
is an illusion not worth pursuing, a limitation
on the imagination's plate. It makes no sense
to her, she says, mimesis and narration
are out of the question, boring, passé, old-fashioned.
She feels a rancor for the empirical. Abstraction,
disjunction, juxtaposition, and all the other *shuns*

take her fancy. And all the friendly stories
of my childhood pack up and walk out the door,
taking with them their pungent oranges, melons, raspberries,
the sweet fruit salad of the juicy familiar,
leaving us with a mouthful of semiotics,
poststructuralism doing its after-dinner tricks.

❧ Les poètes célèbres

I, too, know something about the languid
aestheticism of Paris, the Louvre, the Champs Élysées,
and I can drop the right names—Rimbaud, Mallarmé,
Celan, as good as the next guy. If I said
Tranströmer, Rilke, Wittgenstein, Nietzsche, would
you nod your privileged head and languish with me
in the salon with M, or B, and Valéry
in language as insubstantial as a cloud?

I've been there, spent those sultry nights in Rome
some poets dream on, pretending to be cosmopolitan
with the best of them. But give me Cleveland,
Pittsburgh, Milwaukee, Chicago, and a few good words
like *balderdash, hogwash, flabbergast, hornswoggle, con.*
I'll sing with Whitman of *lickspittle, duds,* and *turds.*

🐝 The McPoem

I must confess that I, too, like it:
the poem that's fried up flat and fast with condiments
on a sesame seed bun. Steamy, grease-spattered,
and juicy, fluent with salt, piping hot
from the grill, glazed with bubbling oil.
A poem you can count on always to be
the same—small, domestic, fun for the whole
family. Economical. American. Free

of culinary pretension. I used to have to ride
ten miles or so out to the suburbs to find
one back in 1956 when poems were
more expensive, reserved for connoisseurs.
Now everyone is welcome to the griddle.
(I also like toads, and all this fiddle.)

❧ Waxworms

Ten below, the sun on the bright horizon
lighting the ice with a blue, uncertain glow.
The old man, in snowmobile suit and earflaps,
says the reason I'm not catching fish is that
my bait is sluggish and cold. He places his thumb
in his cheek and extracts, like a watery chaw of tobacco,
a passel of waxworms, and, with his forefinger, taps
them apart and hands me what looks pretty much like a maggot.

Here, son, he says (although I'm almost fifty),
and slips the rest of the chaw back into his cheek
and returns to his plastic fish bucket and solitary jigging.
There's something about being out on the ice with a crafty
old man, and the things that come out of his mouth! A week
of Sundays couldn't be more spiritually uplifting.

❧ Skin

There's something about the touch of skin on skin—
the handshake, the pat on the back, the arm
around the shoulder, the body's simple terms
of agreement, reassurance, consolation—
that sends an electric buzz to brain and spine,
the blind synapses snapping, full capacity,
to light the body's fires, high on the wine
of camaraderie or love. And if we

find ourselves inhabited by winter,
the mind's blank sky branching nowhere,
snow the best the cold heart can hope for,
buried under time's fraying comforter,
hand on naked back or thigh on thigh
can send us south into the middle of July.

🐾 An Essay on Love

Every morning the cat jumps on my chair
wanting love. She sits and paws the air,
a gesture so endearing and so human,
who could deny her? I stroke and stroke her fur
until it crackles and snaps, electric, and then
I shove her out and lock the heavy door.
I wonder what my small attentions mean
to her? Is it merely what it seems:

stimulus and response; act and reward?
Her blind instinctual claim of territory
leaving the mark of her oily scent on me,
taking whatever payment I can afford?
And what about the rest of us? Is it love
that moves and shakes us? We'd like to think it's love.

❧ Man Sleeping

He lay awake. He tossed and turned. He could
not get to sleep. The place eluded him
as if it were some far-off destination
he'd lost the map to. If the neighbor's lamp would
just go out, the errant leopard frog
stop his protestations, the garish nightjar
leave off celebrating whatever star
it was that burned its hole in sleep's thick bog.

Minutes passed. Hours. It could have been
years. His father gone. His mother. Even his
daughters passed through sleep. The lamp turned off,
the bird, the star, the bright amphibian.
And then they all were gone, these lights of his.
And he, at last, was left with dark enough.

Long for This World:

New Poems

1 ❧ Local Hero

My nickname, growing up, was "Rusty" Wallace—
the same as the race car driver by that name
who roars across the headlines of
The Saint Louis Post Dispatch:
RUSTY WALLACE TRIUMPHS
or **WALLACE WINS AGAIN.**
Oh! say the little old ladies at my mother's church
who remember that small boy fondly—
Joseph in the Christmas pageant,
towing his squeaky donkey down the aisle;
altar boy in surplice and muffled silly grin;
soprano in the choir loft spinning out
his tinny solos in the high-compression air—*Oh!*
You must be proud of him! Such an illustrious career!
The grueling work he's doing—so very dangerous!
All that power and speed, the terrible crashes!
She used to try to explain it wasn't me
on those oversize tires, athwart that throbbing
engine, the packed house hoping for a victory or
a crack-up. How *I* drove only the smaller vehicles—
sonnets and sestinas, villanelles,
though I'd been known
to hazard a bit of fast talk, take a joy ride in
free verse. But they'd have nothing of it: *Oh my,*
you're much too modest. We've seen him race.
On track that man is . . . is . . . pure poetry!
Him and his whole pit crew!
So now my mother smiles and acquiesces: *Yes,*
her son's a winner, after all. And when, on
Easter Sunday, I'm back to visit from
wherever their cheering imaginations would have it,
the aging pastor driving
his old slow message home
about how we'll all be resurrected

at the finish line one day
if we power up our lives with
the high octane of prayer,
his metaphor a nod in my direction,
and I feel all eyes on me,
I'm Rusty Wallace, local hero, NASCAR bard
extraordinaire, fastest goddamn poet on the track!

🐾 The Old West

At the Sonoran Desert Museum
on the edge of the Saguaro National Monument,
that stretch of low hill and arroyo
that every Western movie hero
has ridden his rental horse through,
an elderly woman is crying in the heat.
Her husband is shouting at her
as if she were deaf, *Does she want*
a yogurt, or some nice ice water?
What in God's name is the matter with her
now? But she is lost in the desert
of herself—where every silent saguaro,
every blazing ocotillo, every blossoming
acacia bright as the sun, every thorned
palo verde, every mesquite, every
creosote bush, every small daisy fleabane
looks the same, and every bare patch
of sand and panicky gravel
could be a trail. *Help me,* she shouts
back, uncertain, out of her lost
canyon with its insurmountable boulders
and its dry riverbed. But he's gone
to the hummingbird enclosure, or to see
the seventeen kinds of rattlesnake,
the pack rats and prairie dogs,
the hawks and havalinas. Later, I'll be
in a topless bar in Tucson, drunk
and rowdy as any outlaw, the whole
shabby room abloom with nude girls.
But for now I am the hero, the kindly
town marshal mounting up a posse
to ride out and bring the varmint back
and toss him in the hoosegow
for cruelty to women. *Howdy, Ma'am,*
I offer. Is there something I can do?

❧ Redundancies

I've always wanted to have
backups for everything—
two houses, two cars,
two computers, two kids.
I'd have two wives, two
hearts, if I could. So don't
tell me I can't have
"the aesthetics of beauty"
as the title of the next chapter of
my life. Where beauty is
concerned, I would double
my money, have two
for the price of one.
I've never had a problem
with second chances, second
opinions. The tautology of repetition
has a certain interest, a certain
charm (Got you? Got you again?)
Perhaps it has something to do
with *being,* the ontology of being;
or *knowledge,* the epistemology
of knowledge. Let me repeat,
again: On each diurnal day
I look for some teleology
of purpose. Why not be doubly
satisfied, twice blessed?
I would make a gift of
this present. I would consider
my choice of options. I would
examine the theology of
religion, the inspiration of
breath, the optics of vision.
I would be twice
the man I am.

❧ Literature in the 21st Century

Sometimes I wish I drank coffee
or smoked Marlboros, or maybe cigars—
yes, a hand-rolled Havana cigar
in its thick, manly wrapping,
the flash of the match between
worn matchbook and stained forefinger,
the cup of the palm at the tip,
the intake of air, and the slow and
luxuriant, potent and pleasurable
exhale. Shall we say also a glass
of claret? Or some sherry with its
dark star, the smoke blown into the bowl
of the glass, like fog on a portentous
morning, the rich man-smell of gabardine
and wool, of money in its gold clip?

Sometimes I wish I had habits
a man wouldn't kick, faults a good man could
be proud of. I'd be an expatriate from
myself, all ink–pen and paper in a Paris cafe
where the waiters were elegant and surly,
the women relaxed and extravagant
with their bobbed hair and bonbons, their
perfumed Galoises, their oysters and canapés,
and I'd be writing about war and old losses—
man things—and not where I am, in this
pristine and sensitive vessel, all
fizzy water, reticence, and care, all reduced
fat and purified air, behind my deprived
computer, where I can't manage even
a decaf cap, a mild Tiparillo, a glass of
great-taste-less-filling light beer.

❧ Gas

Here in my old age,
when intestinal gas has become
(how to say it?)
more of a "problem,"
I sometimes wish
the ban on flatulence
could be, by general consent,
universally lifted, and we
would all be free
to relieve ourselves at will.
I mean, why should occasional
coughing be permitted, in even
the most elegant of places—
the opera, say, or the symphony,
or the lecture hall, or church.
Or nose-blowing, or, even, eruc-
tation, if done with delicacy or
a modicum of decorum.
How many times have I sat
in agony, face flushed, in a sweat,
the small cramp in my gut
moving with a mind of its own
as I clenched and unclenched
the sated sphincter muscles,
crossed and uncrossed my legs
as the nearly indistinguishable
muttering of unrelievable pressure
raised its protest, and, preoccupied,
I missed the whole performance?
And would it be disastrous
if everybody, after all, in the
audience, at once, let loose,
all that flammable miasma,
that combustible effluvium,

filling the awkward air.
Oh, I know they say that cows
improbably contribute to global
warming, the greenhouse effect,
all that errant methane,
and would we want to exacerbate
something so serious as that?
But think of the ultimate pleasure
of 200, 500, 1,000 people
farting! The collective letting go,
the contented sigh. The relief,
the comic relief, even, as
our bodies agreed, in harmony,
that yes, we all are human, yes,
despite our classy tuxedoes
our glamorous satin dresses,
our scrubbed and polished faces
and coifed hair, despite our
petty failings, our impossible
aspirations, our eloquence and
bluster, we will all pass
muster, pass gas.

🐚 How Laughter

tripped us up. Slapped us
with his bad jokes, tickled
our childhoods mercilessly.
How anything, once, was funny—
the peekaboo face in the cradle;
the goofy *boop!* on the nose;
the hilarious grade school hijinks:
Rusty Bedsprings by I. P. Knightley;
Brown Wall by Hu Flung Pu.
How laughter, our best friend,
defended us against all possible
disaster so Bobby, the quadriplegic,
could play first base, and the Moron,
our scapegoat, could throw
his clock out the window
to see time fly. Laughter was
the bad boy in church who tickled us
during the silent prayer
or skewered the shapeless matrons
with their blue hair,
or embarrassed the flatulent old men
and added the jazzy punch line as
"the piece that passeth understanding"
popped out of the minister's mouth.
How we tittered and snickered and giggled,
how we chuckled and chortled and roared,
how we simply could not stop laughing
at the world with its straight face.

Now laughter, grown up, polite,
appears at our cocktail parties
in his clever three-piece suit,
or makes a public appearance
at speeches—a brief nod and a wave.

He's no longer contagious—another
defeated childhood disease. We
have laughed till we cried,
inoculated by grief. Now
we're finally immune to merriment.
No one's going to die laughing.

❧ General Fuckup

Why are the bonehead
moments always the closest?
The gaffes, the mistakes, the blunders,
the faux pas and miscues?
You can forget your great successes,
lose the keys or composure
you had just seconds ago,
watch your grandest hours
fade off and go AWOL.
But the goofs, the slips, the lapses,
the idiotic, the asinine,
present themselves on cue
for your tireless inspection—
shoes shined, pants pressed,
standing at attention—
on the parade ground of any
new place you'd like to go.
They're always there saluting you—
Sergeant Dullard, Colonel Dolt,
Admiral Mooncalf, Commander Nitwit—
that loyal band of followers
you always keep in tow.

❧ Failed Poems

What is it about them? The way
they sit in the back of the room, frowning
or gazing off into space, their black
caps pointing them backwards to
wherever it was they came from, as if
any place would be a better place to be.
Dumb jocks, are they, who won't
participate in the recitation, line up,
or sing when the whole world's singing?
Or fast girls the choir boys up front,
in their elegance and polished strut,
are wont to dismiss as sluts?

Slacker, laggard, know-nothing, dunce—
do they *try* to fail, their eyes glazed,
their thick mouths shut? Or do they
just not try hard enough? No matter
how you lead them through the material,
no matter the coaching, the one-on-one,
they just put in their time and then
disappear out of your life,
an empty space at the back of the page,
a blue goose egg in the grade book,
with hardly a thought in the world
for the sad old fart who failed them.

❧ Alas, Thomas Midgley

came up with the idea
of adding lead to gasoline
to make it burn more freely
and propel our sluggish blood,
and then he thought of Freon
to cool us down and heat
the planet up, and then
he contracted polio and
invented a contraption
of slings and ropes and ironies
that finally hung him up,
went awry and strangled him,
his head lost in the ozone,
his body heavy as lead.

🐦 Bird Brain

for Fernando Nottebohm

And yet, a beautiful complex thing
capable of producing such song!
And he loved them and wondered
how it was they learned such singing,
and some even learning, every year,
a *new* song! And so he clipped the
neurons in their right brain, their
left brain, leaving them speechless,
and came up with a theory of
neurogenesis that could benefit us all,
even the tone-deaf among us, who—
no matter how hard we work at it,
dissecting all day long, with our
Peterson Guides and bird tapes—
can grasp but a handful of bird notes,
and can't sing a single song.

❧ The Truth

for Amy

Her breast cancer, she said,
had metastasized to her liver;
she was going to die, and
soon. She said it made her
sad. I didn't know her well.
We were co-workers and
I liked her, but
what do you say when someone
actually answers the question
how are you?
with the unvarnished truth:
Not well, she said. *I haven't
long to live.* And should I
have said *Oh you will!* Should I
have smoothed it over
with the syrup of nervousness,
or done what I did
which was to
talk about terror and anger,
the unfairness and the lie,
to take the truth at face value?
No, she was just sad, she said.
She had her faith, she said,
and started to cry. And only then
did I see what she needed from me
was miracle, a simple belief
in miracle, and if that was varnish,
well, it would bring the grain
of the truth out, would save it
from wear and weather.
It would make the truth
almost shine.

❧ The Physical

For starters, she is beautiful.
Dark and Lebanese. She's
touched his hands and feet,
lingered over
his ears, and nose, and throat.
And here he is in his underwear,
flat on the examining table, as she
snaps her latex gloves. He's
wondering whether he'll keep his
cool or rise to the occasion.
The room is steel and antiseptic,
sterile and fluorescent, but
there's something about her uniform—
where's the starchy polyester, the sensible
brassiere?—and the way
her dark eyes sparkle
under her swept-back hair
that gives him pause.
In any other circumstance, he thinks,
this would be pleasure,
her hand inside his pants now,
her middle finger lubricated,
the old electric buzz.
And how are your wife and daughters?
she says, and suddenly it's
rectal and testicular, Latinate and
detached, a pat examination of
dispassionate body parts.
And then she's done, and the hard
part's over, is it not?
He wonders if she's come
to any conclusions,
as she turns her back on him
and clucks her dangerous tongue.

No Deal

And when I died, the devil came and said,
"Now here's the deal: I'll give you your old life
all over once again, no strings attached.
Like an actor in a play, of course, you'll have
to follow the same script that you rehearsed
the first time through—you cannot change a glance,
a word, a gesture; but think of taking your first
steps again, and having your first romance

repeat itself, your love back from the dead,
beautiful and new and seventeen.
What matter if you see the future coming—
the cloven hoof of sorrow, loss's horn—
in her dreamy eye, her nodding head?"
Get thee behind me, Satan, I should have said.

Claustrophobia

probably isn't the word for it:
this ancient desperate longing
to escape the confines of loss.
It's not the *size* of the room,
it's not even a *room*, exactly—
this place where the past should gather,
holding hands, all your former selves
that went off on their own,
despite you, never to come home.

What kind of friend is memory,
constantly reminding you of who
and what you're not, turning love
into cells and synapses? Sometimes,
it seems, the only friend you've got.

2 ❦ The Face of God

Today, on my marathon run,
the March air cold and sunny,
the ground still frozen, trees
bare, the ice on the lake breaking
up, tinkling like wind chimes, all
promise and possibility, I saw—or rather
sensed in the cold sweat on my chest,
the heavy feet, the side stitch and labored
breathing—the Face of God: Not the God
of my dead father; not my grandfather's
Sunday God as he celebrated on the pump
organ, stern but endurable; not the
anthropomorphic gentleman my mother
and grandmother loved, the God of
Peace that Passeth Understanding;
what I saw was less a face than a
miasma—huge, alien, omnipresent—
as pleased with evil as with
good; as much a virus as
a cure, a Hitler as a Christ;
cosmic dust; a black hole; the cold and
gaseous planets; the billion billion
unsentient suns; in short the face
of facelessness, indifference, the
unimaginably *beyond.* The vision hovered
the way certain chords in Bach chorales
hover on the edge of redemption, of
unendurable longing, sexual tension,
seemingly irresolvable, out of reach,
as if the piano or the life
needed tuning, the hammer set to stretch
the errant wire into a pitch past pitch
of joy or sorrow where the mind and heart

could sever, could snap, the sated flesh
collapse, the lemony tongue turn dumb . . .
until the final chord comes
sending us back into our bodies,
and the bright cold world runs on.

🐾 Shoes

> One shoe, two shoes, a dozen shoes, yes. But how can you
> describe several thousand shoes?
> *Edward R. Murrow*

At the Holocaust Museum in Washington, D.C.,
between the video histories and photo tableaux,
this slag heap, this lava flow, of shoes:
Old shoes, tired shoes, lost shoes, abandoned shoes,
an industrial rubble of shoes. Saddle shoes, buckle shoes,
tie shoes, high-button shoes, wing tips, cap-toes, loafers, flats.
Open-toe and closed-toe shoes, baby shoes, grannie shoes,
high-heeled shoes, low-heeled shoes, well-heeled shoes,
broken shoes, oxfords, sandals, brogues, taps.
Shoes without their mates. Overshoes, winter shoes,
summer shoes, all-season shoes, shoes that have seen
better days, shoes with their eyes on the future,
hopeful shoes. Left shoes, right shoes, formal shoes,
leisure shoes, shoes for all occasions, work shoes, party
shoes, a pollution, an ash heap, an hallucination of shoes.
Fashionable and unfashionable shoes. Practical shoes,
hiking shoes, dress shoes, casual shoes, suede shoes,
cordovans, shit-kickers, monk-straps, pumps.
Shoes with their tongues cut out, mute shoes, deaf
shoes, shoes with their eyelets ripped, soleless shoes,
shoes that will never again take up their laces and walk.
Leather shoes, cloth shoes, cheap shoes, expensive shoes,
a mass grave, a wasteland, a moonscape of shoes.

> Shoe (shoo) n. 1. A durable covering for the human foot.
> 2. A part or device that functions as a protective covering.
> 3. A device that retards or stops the motion of an object.
> 4. A chute, as for conveying grain from a hopper.
> 5. Shoes. *Informal.* a. Position; status: *You*
> *would understand my decision if you put yourself in my shoes.*
> b. Plight: *I wouldn't want to be in her shoes.*

If the shoe fits shoes. Waiting for the other shoe to drop shoes.
Nobody's shoes. Somebody's shoes. Anybody's shoes. Everybody's shoes.

❧ Photo from Liberia

A piece of leg, with mummified skin,
bronze, mahogany. Where the foot had been,

a dirty sock, looking for all the world
as if it still contained a foot. Curled

like fingernail clippings, ribs scatter
the available light in the patterns

of a body: pubis, vertebrae, the smear
of what was once the other leg, fear

in the deep eye sockets of the skull,
jaw agape as if still trying to call

out, lying on its side, and pinned
there by some unseen alien hand.

The dirt and gravel road a dull montage
of mottled brown and green camouflage,

the earth's fatigues. As if asleep,
at intervals, in blank repose, one heap

of bones after another. A white shred
of underwear, a blue robe—the dead's

preposterous clothes. On the airstrip,
flashing their fleshy hand and lip,

likewise camouflaged in brown and green,
soldiers, laced with ammo, machine

guns pointed at the wide, indifferent sky,
supremely undisturbed, as if to die

were singularly uninteresting, stare
out at us, serene. Arrested, we stare

back at them from our safe country far
away. Or maybe not so far.

Sayonara

Her first time fishing. Fumiko
flails with the open-faced reel,
spin-casting expletives: *Shi! Shi!*
As I help her unsnarl I tell her
I speak no Japanese. *Oh, yes!*
she sings in lilting English.
Sushi. Tofu. Toyota.
A smile behind her hand.

This is New Zealand, Lake Agnes.
West coast. A wooden boat.
In the beeches, bellbirds.
The blue and green kea's cry.
Tree ferns and Spanish moss.
In part of the sky it is raining.
In part, sun. A larceny
of ripples on the water.

Earlier in the day, a Kiwi
on the track complained
that foreigners were ruining
his country. Logging. Resorts.
Now Fumiko's getting the hang of it,
trout piling up like silver pillage.
She bows to each of them:
I am so sorry. I am so sorry.

Sayonara, she smiles at me,
and thwacks them on the back.

❧ The Invasion of the Body Snatchers

wasn't just a movie, after all,
a cold war childhood nightmare
that scared us, it turns out, to death.
The terror that landed so long ago
is real. One by one they
come for us, bending us double,
gouging our eyes out,
rotting our teeth,
breaking our hips and knees.
Our bodies are no fit
place for them, and yet
come they must, stealing
our memories and dreams,
making us strangers
to ourselves, as we grow
hopeless and alien, frightening
the children, losing our way.
And what can we do, as they
become our grandparents and parents,
our friends and neighbors and spouses,
but sequester them in condos and
assisted care facilities, and wait
for the seed pods hidden in
the closets of our DNA,
the deep recesses of our genes,
the storerooms of our cells,
to raise their ugly heads,
to surface and absorb us.

🐾 Hey Buddy, Need a Lift?

Happiness, fat and wheezy,
puffs up in his pickup truck, all smiles,
beside himself with Joy. They're
loud; it sounds like they've been
drinking. He wants me
to get in. *Come on!* he shouts,
flashing his glad hand.
The truck's filled up
with the day's accumulations
of luck, windfalls, found money—
a jumbled concatenation stacked
in the flatbed. I can just make out
a rusty grin; a cockeyed pile of
twinkles; a jig, a guffaw, a chuckle.
He's a tinker, a junkman, a rag picker;
he'll make something of it,
he'll sell it if he can.
Get in! he calls again, although
there's hardly room for me with my
heavy heart, my satchel full of woe,
my lifetime supply of sorrow.
He wants me to *give it up,*
to leave it all behind—my belongings,
my prized possessions—to
let go! to *travel light! Last chance,*
he calls, *Get in!* The truck revs up
its engine. I suppose I could
take a chance on Happiness,
I suppose I could jump for Joy.
It's true I could use a lift.
But didn't my mother always tell me
never to talk to strangers?
And do I really want to
get taken for a ride?

🐾 On Prozac

So much happiness! It seems
everything I touch shines back, all smiles.
Sadness, that old sot, has packed his bags;
sorrow's folded up her tents, moved on;
anger's banished. What more
could any monarch hope for?

But is this what I wanted, after all?

Sufficiency, serenity, and pleasure
always at my table, in my bed?
What do you do with such a glittering world
that has no room for what you once held dear?
And who will teach me now
to spin straw back from all this heavy gold?

SmackDown!

It's all an act, isn't it?
When Love gets up and struts its stuff,
flexing its pecs and biceps,
its gaudy, improbable muscles,
we all know it's choreographed, fake.
So when the ringside announcer claims
Kid Valentine's all heart
and Captain Romance is,
and has always been, champ,
we know better. We're no country
bumpkins, we weren't born yesterday,
you can't put that stuff
over on us, we say, as we
sit back on our haunches and scoff.
But wait! Why's that tag team,
Desire and Lust, thrusting its attributes
out at us, taunting us, mouthing off?
And why is the camera now swiveling—
Oh my!—its bright eye in our direction?
We're too old for such foolishness,
we think, but—*Good Lord!*—you're
the babe in the too-tight tank top, I'm
the hunk in the red satin trunks,
and we're up out of our seats now,
all cartoon breasts & sequins,
all forearms & crotch,
all latex & spandex & pomp,
wondering just how we got here,
and who's got the script,
and will we luck out,
and get smacked down for the count?

In the Virgin Islands

Sunset: a smattering of rain
on the tent flap; a bananaquit flashes
like a lit match, and vanishes.
And now the night starts up
its grand concatenations: insects
natter at the bug lamp;
tree frogs peep and chortle
as if tickled at their good fortune
to be living so far south, in winter.

This is what travel gives us—
the promise that, no matter
the landscapes of absence,
the absolute zero of silence,
the deaths and exits we must tender,

somewhere pelicans are
roosting in palm fronds,
frigate birds are riding the updrafts,
and someone as dim
as a bananaquit or tree frog
has something important to sing about
and all the warm night to sing it in.

❧ Lucky

He was a lucky bastard.
He had the luck of the Irish,
was lucky at love.
It was just his luck.
He had kissed the blarney stone,
stroked the rabbit's foot,
found the four-leaf clover,
touched the hunchback's hump.
He thanked his lucky stars
he always lucked into things,
lucked out. No matter how
he tried or pushed his,
his luck never changed
or ran in streaks; it held.
He was always in luck.
When other people were
down on theirs, calling his
dumb or blind, he knew his
luck was pure. He wished
them it, for all the good it
did them; it was just his.
And if his days were numbered,
when his number came up, well,
it was his lucky day:
luck was a lady that night;
he got lucky.
He was a lucky stiff,
as luck would have it.

❧ Pleasure

according to Freud, requires
the build-up and release of
tension. And so
this bitter December day,
the temperature below
below, could be the beginning
of pleasure: wind zipped
to the face; digits vegetal, chill;
can we talk about
finger food? Talk about
bone? In the land of
less is more,
hopeless is *hope* plus
less; there's sun in the snow,
an air in the air; no need
for a mirror to
check for your breath.
The cold
keeps you moving

deep south to summer—its
ibises, egrets, its sea foam
abroil with sheepshead and
mullet. O fish that can fly!
Sweet mildew! O lovely
palmetto! How opposites
attract, pleasure each other.
Another thing death is
the mother of. Pleasure!
With some people,
it's a principle.

❧ Blessings

occur.
Some days I find myself
putting my foot in
the same stream twice;
leading a horse to water
and making him drink.
I have a clue.
I can see the forest
for the trees.

All around me people
are making silk purses
out of sows' ears,
getting blood from turnips,
building Rome in a day.
There's a business
like show business.
There's something new
under the sun.

Some days misery
no longer loves company;
it puts itself out of its.
There's rest for the weary.
There's turning back.
There are guarantees.
I can be serious.
I can mean that.
You can quite
put your finger on it.

Some days I know
I am long for this world.
I can go home again.
And when I go
I can
take it with me.

🐦 Acknowledgments

The new poems included here were originally published in the following magazines: *Connecticut Review:* "Photo from Liberia," and "Sayonara"; *5 a.m.:* "Failed Poems"; *The Formalist:* "No Deal"; *The Laurel Review:* "The Physical"; *Margie:* "Redundancies"; *Ontario Review:* "The Truth"; *Paris Review:* "On Prozac"; *Poem* 80 (1998): "Claustrophobia"; *Poetry:* "Bird Brain," "Pleasure," and "Smack-Down!"; *Poetry Northwest:* "Alas, Thomas Midgley," "Blessings," "Hey Buddy, Need a Lift?" "Lucky," and "Shoes"; *Sewanee Review,* vol. 109, no. 2 (spring 2001): "The Face of God"; *Southern Review:* "Literature in the 21st Century"; *Sou'wester:* "Local Hero"; *Tar River Poetry:* "General Fuckup"; *Virginia Quarterly Review* 73.2 (1997): "How Laughter" and "The Old West."

The selected poems included here originally appeared in *Plums, Stones, Kisses & Hooks* (University of Missouri Press, 1981), *Tunes for Bears to Dance To* (University of Pittsburgh Press, 1983), *People and Dog in the Sun* (University of Pittsburgh Press, 1987), *The Makings of Happiness* (University of Pittsburgh Press, 1991), *Time's Fancy* (University of Pittsburgh Press, 1994), and *The Uses of Adversity* (University of Pittsburgh Press, 1998), and in the following magazines: *Blue Moon Review, Cedar Rock, Chelsea, Chowder Review, Cincinnati Poetry Review, Crazy Horse, The Cream City Review, The Formalist, The Gettysburg Review, The Iowa Review, Kentucky Poetry Review, The Laurel Review, Licking River Review, The Little Magazine, The Madison Review, New Letters, The New Yorker, Poet and Critic, Poet Lore, Poetry, Poetry Northwest, Prairie Schooner, The Southern Review, Southwest Review, Sou'Wester, Tar River Poetry, Yankee.*

Special thanks to Vivian Kiechel of Vivian Kiechel Fine Art of Lincoln, Nebraska, for permission to use John Steuart Curry's *Rainbow and View of Madison, Wisconsin* as cover art.

Ronald Wallace is Felix Pollak Professor of Poetry at the University of Wisconsin–Madison where he codirects the creative writing program and serves as general editor for the University of Wisconsin Press poetry series. He is the author of eleven books, including the poetry collections *The Makings of Happiness, Time's Fancy,* and *The Uses of Adversity;* the short story collection *Quick Bright Things;* and the critical study *God Be With the Clown: Humor in American Poetry.* He is married and has two grown daughters, and divides his time between Madison and a forty-acre farm in Bear Valley, Wisconsin.